From Pause to Purpose

Empowering Devotions for the Unemployed

Jennifer Francis

Copyright © 2025 by Jennifer Francis

All rights reserved. No part of this publication may be reproduced, distributed, or transmitted in any form or by any means, including photocopying, recording, or other electronic or mechanical methods, without the prior written permission of the author, except in the case of brief quotations embodied in critical reviews and certain other noncommercial uses permitted by copyright law.

Scripture quotations marked (AMP) are taken from the Amplified® Bible (AMP), Copyright © 2015 by The Lockman Foundation. Used by permission. Scripture quotations marked (NLT) are taken from the Holy Bible, New Living Translation, copyright © 1996, 2004, 2015 by Tyndale House Foundation. Used by permission of Tyndale House Publishers, Inc. All rights reserved. Scripture quotations marked (NKJV) are taken from the New King James Version®. Copyright © 1982 by Thomas Nelson. Used by permission. All rights reserved. Scripture quotations marked (NIV) are taken from the Holy Bible, New International Version®, NIV®. Copyright © 1973, 1978, 1984, 2011 by Biblica, Inc.™ Used by permission of Zondervan. All rights reserved worldwide. www.zondervan.com The "NIV" and "New International Version" are trademarks registered in the United States Patent and Trademark Office by Biblica, Inc.™ Scripture quotations marked (MSG) are taken from THE MESSAGE, copyright © 1993, 2002, 2018 by Eugene H. Peterson. Used by permission of NavPress. All rights reserved. Represented by Tyndale House Publishers, Inc. Scripture quotations marked (TPT) are from The Passion Translation®. Copyright © 2017, 2018, 2020 by Passion & Fire Ministries, Inc. Used by permission. All rights reserved. ThePassionTranslation.com. Scripture quotations marked (CSB) are taken from the Christian Standard Bible®, Copyright © 2017 by Holman Bible Publishers. Used by permission. Christian Standard Bible® and CSB® are federally registered trademarks of Holman Bible Publishers, all rights reserved.

ISBN: 979-8-218-66345-2
First Edition: 2025
Printed in the USA
FromPause2Purpose.com

Dedication

To the Holy Spirit, my ever-present Senior Partner, You've been my guiding light through every twist and turn of this journey called life. Your whispers remind me daily that I'm never alone, even when the path seems unclear.

To my family, Nando, Ellen, Guille, Rhonda, Dito, Natalie, Dorian, Kaya, Lydia, Devin, Nia, Najee, Maria, Jill, Vicky, and Mishy, thank you for embodying the true essence of family - being present in my life's joyous peaks and challenging valleys. Your unwavering support during both my celebratory and somber moments has been the cornerstone of my journey. You are my anchors in the storm and companions in the sunshine. Thank you for being the true definition and example of family.

To my husband Yusuf, yours is the hand I hold when the world spins too fast, the laughter that brightens my darkest days, and the voice of reassurance when doubt creeps in. Your faith and love constantly remind me that God is with me, God is for me, God is fighting for me, and God has my front and back ... God got me.

To Pastor Jimmy Talton and Lady Daisy Talton, thank you for your spiritual guidance and support, which have been a constant source of strength and inspiration. Your teachings and prayers have enriched my faith and illuminated my path. You both serve as true role models in my life and exemplify how to walk by faith.

Contents

Introduction VI

How to Use This Devotional VII

When Life Hits the Pause Button 1

The Ultimate Safety Net 5

Recharging Your Inner Battery 9

When Dreams Get Derailed 13

The Art of Sacred Downtime 17

GPS for the Soul 21

Kicking Anxiety to the Curb 25

Mastering the 24/7 Hustle 29

Building Your Bounce-Back Muscles 33

Your Spiritual Dream Team 37

Leveling Up in Life 41

God's Perfect Timing in an Instant World 45

Flipping the Script on Negativity 49

Money Matters: Divine Edition 53

Riding the Waves of Change 57

The Dignity of All Work 61

Navigating Family Dynamics 65

The Waiting Game: God's Perspective 69

Redefining Your Win 73

Bouncing Back from the "No" 77

Finding Joy in the Journey 81

Networking with Purpose 85

Overcoming Self-Doubt 89

The Importance of Self-Care 93

Serving Others While Unemployed 97

Staying Motivated in the Job Search 101

Balancing Persistence and Flexibility 105

Breaking Free from the Comparison Trap 109

Prepped and Ready for What's Next 113

Gratitude: Your Secret Weapon 117

Turning the Page: Your Next Chapter Begins 121

About The Author 125

Introduction

In the challenging journey of unemployment, faith can often feel like a flickering flame amid a storm of uncertainty. I know this firsthand. After twenty years at a corporation, I woke up one day to realize there was no job to go to. Thoughts bombarded me concerning every aspect of my life. "Where do I go from here? Why did this happen? What's next, God?" These questions became my constant companions.

This devotional is born from that experience. It's designed to be your daily companion, offering a beacon of hope and a foundation of strength as you navigate these uncharted waters. Each reflection is carefully crafted to address the unique emotional, spiritual, and practical challenges unemployment brings while firmly anchoring you in the timeless truths of Scripture. Whether you're facing your first day without a job or have been searching for months, these pages aim to remind you of God's unwavering presence and purpose in your life.

As you embark on this journey, remember that this is more than just a book; it's an invitation to transformation. Each devotion offers biblical insights to ground you in God's truth, reflective questions to deepen your understanding, practical action steps to apply what you've learned, and declarations to meditate on. Through these elements, this devotional seeks to comfort you in your present circumstances and equip you for a future filled with hope and purpose.

How to Use This Devotional

Set aside a specific time each day for your reading and reflection. Read the passage slowly and thoughtfully. Take time to answer the reflective questions, perhaps in a journal. Commit to the daily action step. Meditate on the declarations throughout your day.

Remember, your worth is not defined by your employment status but by your identity as a beloved child of God. May these words inspire you to approach each day with renewed faith, resilience, and expectation, knowing God is working in and through your circumstances.

As you begin this journey, trust that God has a purpose for this season and that He is faithful to complete the good work He has started in you.

When Life Hits the Pause Button

"Then you will experience God's peace, which exceeds anything we can understand. His peace will guard your hearts and minds as you live in Christ Jesus." (Philippians 4:7, NLT)

When unemployment hits, it often feels like someone has abruptly pressed the pause button on your life. The steady rhythm of work, income, and purpose suddenly screeches to a halt, leaving you in a whirlwind of uncertainty and anxiety. In these moments, we need something to steady us that's more powerful than our own understanding. We need God's supernatural peace.

This verse promises a peace that surpasses our understanding. Peace is not the absence of trouble but a profound calm in the midst of the storm. This divine peace acts as a guardian, protecting our hearts from despair and our minds from spiraling into worst-case scenarios.

Living "in Christ Jesus" is the key to accessing this peace. It means staying connected to Him through prayer, meditating on His Word, and trusting His promises. When financial worries threaten to overwhelm you, this peace reminds you that your job status doesn't define your worth. When the future seems uncertain, it assures you that God holds your tomorrow.

This peace doesn't just soothe; it empowers. It gives you the clarity to make wise decisions about your next steps. It provides the strength to face each day with hope rather than dread. It offers a testimony to others of God's faithfulness in your life, even in challenging times.

Instead of frantically trying to restart your life, take a moment to experience God's peace. Let it wash over your anxious thoughts about job applications, interviews, and financial pressures. Allow it to guard your heart against discouragement and your mind against negativity.

Reflection

How can you practically invite God's peace into your unemployment situation today?

Action Step

Create a "Peace Corner" in your home, a dedicated space where you can retreat to pray, meditate on scripture, and remind yourself of God's faithfulness.

Declarations

- God's peace guards my heart and mind, even in uncertainty.
- I choose to trust in God's plan for my life, including my career.
- My worth is not defined by my employment status but by God's love for me.

Prayer

Heavenly Father, in the midst of this unexpected pause in my career, I come to You seeking the peace that exceeds all understanding. When anxiety about my future threatens to overwhelm me, help me to remember that Your peace is standing guard over my heart and mind.

Lord, I choose to live in Christ Jesus today. Help me stay connected to You, trusting in Your promises and presence. When I'm tempted to frantically search for solutions, remind me first to seek Your peace. Guide me in creating moments of stillness where I can experience Your calming presence.

Thank You for Your peace, which is more powerful than any circumstance I face. Use this season to deepen my trust in You and to demonstrate Your faithfulness in my life. May Your supernatural peace be a testimony to others of Your goodness and care.

In Jesus name I pray, Amen.

The Ultimate Safety Net

"And my God shall supply all your need according to His riches in glory by Christ Jesus." (Philippians 4:19, NKJV)

Unemployment strikes with the force of a sudden earthquake, shaking the very foundation of financial security. As bills stack up and sleepless nights become routine, worrying about making ends meet can overwhelm your thoughts. In these moments of uncertainty, today's verse reminds us of an incredible promise: God Himself is our ultimate safety net.

This scripture doesn't just suggest God might meet our needs or take care of some of them. It boldly declares that He "shall supply all your need." This comprehensive promise covers not just our material needs but our emotional, spiritual, and relational needs as well. When you're unemployed, you need more than just money. You need hope, purpose, wisdom, and strength. God promises to supply all of these.

Notice the standard by which God supplies: "according to His riches in glory." The job market, the economy, or your qualifications do not limit God's resources. His supply comes from His infinite riches in glory. This truth means that even when your bank account is dwindling, you can bank on God's unlimited resources.

This promise doesn't negate the need for action on our part. We still need to be diligent in our job search, wise in our financial decisions, and open to new opportunities. But it does mean that as we do our part, we can trust God to do what only He can do.

Reflection

How has God provided for you in unexpected ways during this season of unemployment?

Action Step

Start a "Provision Journal." Each day, write down at least one way you've experienced God's care, no matter how small it might seem.

Declarations

- God is my ultimate provider, and He knows and will meet my every need.
- I choose to trust in God's abundant riches rather than focus on my current lack.
- Through Christ, I have access to all of God's resources for this season of my life.

Prayer

Heavenly Father, thank You for Your promise to supply all my needs according to Your glorious riches. In times when my resources seem scarce and my future uncertain, help me trust in Your abundant provision. Open my eyes to see the many ways You're caring for me daily.

Lord, give me wisdom to steward well what You've given me and faith to trust You for what I lack. Help me remember that my circumstances do not limit Your supply but flow from Your infinite riches in glory. Guide me to be a good steward of the resources You provide.

As I seek employment, direct my steps and provide for my physical, emotional, and spiritual needs. May my confidence in Your provision be a testimony of Your faithfulness to others. Thank You that in Christ, I have access to all I need for life and godliness.

In Jesus name I pray, Amen.

Recharging Your Inner Battery

"But those who wait for the Lord [who expect, look for, and hope in Him] will gain new strength and renew their power; They will lift up their wings [and rise up close to God] like eagles [rising toward the sun]; They will run and not become weary, They will walk and not grow tired." (Isaiah 40:31, AMP)

It's easy to feel drained and depleted in the midst of unemployment. The constant job searching, dealing with rejection, and facing uncertainty can wear you down. Your inner battery, once charged with purpose and direction, may feel dangerously low. But this verse offers a powerful promise of renewal for those who wait on the Lord.

This isn't passive waiting. It's an active expectation, looking for and hoping in God. It's about shifting your focus from your circumstances to the One who holds your future. As you turn your attention to Him, He promises to renew your strength and power. Like an eagle soaring effortlessly on updrafts, God lifts you above your circumstances, giving you a new perspective and fresh energy.

The image of running without weariness and walking without fatigue speaks to the endurance God provides. He doesn't just offer a quick burst of energy but sustained strength for the long journey ahead. This endurance is crucial in the job search process, which often feels like a marathon rather than a sprint.

Remember, your strength doesn't come from your own resources or abilities but from the infinite power of God. As you wait on Him, you're not wasting time. You're investing it. You're allowing God to recharge, prepare, and equip you for the journey ahead.

Reflection

How can you create more space to "wait on the Lord" and recharge your inner battery in your day?

Action Step

Set aside a specific time each day this week dedicated to waiting on God through prayer, Scripture reading, or quiet reflection.

Declarations

- As I wait on God, He renews my strength for the journey ahead.
- God's power sustains me, even when the job search feels exhausting.
- I rise above my circumstances, gaining new perspective through God's strength.

Prayer

Heavenly Father, in this season of unemployment, I come to You seeking renewal. My inner battery feels depleted, but I trust in Your promise to give new strength to those who wait on You. Help me to wait expectantly, looking for Your work in my life.

Lord, lift me above my circumstances like an eagle soaring on the wind. When the job search feels overwhelming, remind me that Your power is made perfect in my weakness. Give me the endurance to run this race without growing weary and to walk this path without fainting.

Thank You for Your promise of renewed power. As I face each day, help me to draw strength from You. May this time of waiting become a period of spiritual growth and deepened trust in Your faithfulness. Recharge my inner battery with Your love, peace, and hope.

In Jesus name I pray, Amen.

When Dreams Get Derailed

"For I know the plans I have for you,' declares the Lord, 'plans to prosper you and not to harm you, plans to give you hope and a future." (Jeremiah 29:11, NIV)

A job loss shatters the carefully constructed blueprint of life. The career path you envisioned, the goals you set, the future you planned suddenly all seem to veer off course. In these moments, disappointment can be a heavy companion, weighing down your spirit and clouding your vision for the future.

But here's the thing about derailed dreams: they don't have to be the end of the story. This verse reminds us that God has plans for us that go beyond our current circumstances or setbacks. His plans are for our welfare, not for harm. They're designed to give us a future filled with hope, even when our present seems bleak.

This doesn't mean the disappointment isn't real or doesn't hurt. It absolutely does. But it does mean that this derailment isn't final. God can use this unexpected turn to direct you toward something even better than you had imagined. What looks like a roadblock might actually be a redirection to a path more aligned with God's purposes for your life.

Allow yourself to acknowledge the disappointment, but don't camp there. Instead, open your hands and heart to the possibility that God might be using this situation to align you with His greater purposes. Your dreams may be taking a detour, but with God as your guide, the destination might just exceed your wildest expectations.

Remember, God's plans for you are rooted in His perfect knowledge and infinite love for you. He sees the bigger picture and is working all things together for your good, even when you can't see it yet.

Reflection

How might God be using this career setback to reshape your dreams and align them with His purposes?

Action Step

Write a letter to God expressing your disappointment, but also your willingness to trust His plan. End the letter by asking Him to reveal the next step on this new path.

Declarations

- God's plans for me are good, even when my path takes unexpected turns.
- I choose to view this setback as a setup for something greater.
- My hope is anchored in God's promises, not in my circumstances.

Prayer

Heavenly Father, I come to You with a heart heavy with disappointment. My dreams seem to be slipping away, and I'm struggling to understand why. Thank You for Your promise that You have good plans for me, plans to give me hope and a future.

Help me to trust You even when I can't see the road ahead. Give me the courage to let go of my own plans and embrace the journey You have for me. When disappointment threatens to overwhelm me, remind me of Your faithfulness and perfect love.

Lord, I ask for wisdom to see the opportunities in this setback. Open my eyes to the new doors You might be opening and give me the strength to walk through them. Renew my hope and help me to dream new dreams aligned with Your will for my life.

In Jesus name I pray, Amen.

The Art of Sacred Downtime

"Are you tired? Worn out? Burned out on religion? Come to me. Get away with me and you'll recover your life. I'll show you how to take a real rest." (Matthew 11:28, MSG)

In our productivity-obsessed world, "unemployment" can feel like a dirty word. The pressure to constantly be doing something such as sending out resumes, networking, and upgrading skills can be overwhelming. But what if this unexpected downtime is actually a sacred invitation from God? Jesus calls out to those who are weary and burdened, offering not just a quick break but a chance to recover their lives.

This rest isn't about binge-watching your favorite shows or sleeping in (though there's a time for those, too). It's about finding restoration in God's presence. It's a chance to shed the weight of constant doing and embrace the gift of being: being still, being loved, being renewed.

Jesus promises to show us how to take a "real rest." "Real" implies there's a type of rest we often miss, one that goes beyond physical relaxation and touches our souls. It's a rest that rejuvenates not just our bodies but our minds, emotions, and spirits.

Resist the urge to fill every moment with job searching or skill-building. Instead, view this time as a unique opportunity to deepen your relationship with God. Let Him refresh your soul, realign your priorities, and prepare you for the next chapter of your life.

Consider establishing a daily practice of sacred downtime. The form could be a time of prayer, meditation on scripture, or simply sitting in God's presence. Allow yourself to be still and know that He is God, trusting that this time of rest is just as productive as your most active job-seeking efforts.

Reflection

How can you make your downtime more intentional and spiritually refreshing?

Action Step

Create a 'rest ritual': a daily practice that helps you connect with God and find true restoration.

Declarations

- I embrace this season as an opportunity for spiritual growth and renewal.
- My worth is not determined by my productivity but by God's love for me.
- As I rest in God's presence, He is preparing me for what's next.

Prayer

Loving Father, in a world that glorifies busyness, I come to You seeking true rest. Thank You for this invitation to lay my burdens down and find renewal in Your presence. Help me see this period of unemployment not as wasted time but as a sacred opportunity to grow closer to You.

Teach me the art of resting in Your love, trusting in Your provision, and finding peace in Your presence. When I'm tempted to fill every moment with activity, remind me of the value of sacred downtime. Show me how to use this season to realign my priorities with Your will.

Lord, as I learn to embrace this sacred downtime, renew my mind, restore my soul, and refresh my spirit. Use this season to prepare me for Your plans for my future. May I emerge from this time closer to You and more equipped for the journey ahead.

In Jesus name I pray, Amen.

GPS for the Soul

"Trust in the Lord completely, and do not rely on your own opinions. With all your heart rely on him to guide you, and he will lead you in every decision you make." (Proverbs 3:5-6, TPT)

Unemployment blankets your path in a thick fog, making each step uncertain and direction unclear. Which direction should you go? What's the correct next step? It's easy to get overwhelmed by all the options or lack thereof. This scripture offers us a divine GPS for our souls, a guidance system that never fails.

Trusting in the Lord "completely" means letting go of the need to control every aspect of your job search and future career. It's about surrendering your opinions and preconceived notions about how things should work out. Instead, God calls us to rely on Him with all our hearts, not just a part of them.

This reliance isn't passive. It involves actively seeking God's guidance in every decision. It means bringing our job applications, interview opportunities, and career dilemmas before Him. As we do this, He promises to lead us and make our paths straight even when the road ahead seems twisted and unclear.

Instead of trying to map out your entire future, focus on following God's guidance one step at a time. He may not show you the whole journey, but He'll always illuminate the next step. Trust His navigation, even when the route seems unfamiliar or challenging.

Remember, God's GPS for your soul takes into account factors you can't see or understand. He knows your gifts, your potential, and the plans He has for you. By trusting His guidance, you're tapping into divine wisdom that far exceeds any human career advice or strategy.

Reflection

In what areas of your job search do you need to trust God more fully?

Action Step

Before making any job-related decisions today, pause and ask God for His guidance. Write down any insights you receive.

Declarations

- God's wisdom surpasses my understanding, and I choose to trust His guidance.
- I acknowledge God in every aspect of my job search and career planning.
- As I follow God's lead, He is making my path straight.

Prayer

Heavenly Father, I confess that I often try to figure everything out on my own. Thank You for being my divine GPS, always ready to guide me in the right direction. Help me to trust You completely, especially when the path ahead seems unclear.

Give me the courage to let go of my limited understanding and to lean wholly on Your infinite wisdom. Show me how to bring every decision before You, from the smallest task to the biggest career move. When I'm tempted to rely on my own opinions, remind me of Your promise to lead me.

Lord, I acknowledge You in every aspect of my job search and career journey. Please make my paths straight. Show me the next step I should take, and give me the faith to follow Your leading, even when it doesn't make sense to me.

In Jesus name I pray, Amen.

Kicking Anxiety to the Curb

"Do not be anxious or worried about anything, but in everything [every circumstance and situation] by prayer and petition with thanksgiving, continue to make your [specific] requests known to God." (Philippians 4:6, AMP)

Unemployment can be an anxiety-producing pressure cooker. Bills keep coming, savings dwindle, and the financial future looks uncertain. It's like being on a roller coaster you never bought a ticket for, and anxiety is often the unwelcome companion on this ride. But here's the game-changer: you have a direct line to the God of the universe, and He's inviting you to offload your anxieties onto Him.

This verse isn't saying you should never feel anxious; it's giving you a powerful strategy for when anxiety strikes. The antidote to anxiety isn't just positive thinking. It's prayer. Not a formal, stiff kind of prayer, but a real, raw conversation with God. Pour out your heart to Him. Tell Him about the bills, the failed interviews, the dwindling savings.

But don't stop there. Notice the phrase "with thanksgiving". Gratitude has a way of shifting our perspective from what we lack to what we have. Even while unemployed, there are things for which you can be thankful. The support of a friend, a roof over your head, or simply the breath in your lungs are such examples.

The instruction to make your "specific requests known to God" is crucial. God wants to hear the details of your situation. He's interested in every aspect of your job search, every bill that needs paying, every fear that keeps you up at night.

Today, whenever anxiety tries to take hold, use it as a trigger to pray. Turn your worried thoughts into conversations with God. He's listening. He cares. And He's big enough to handle whatever makes you anxious.

Reflection

What specific anxieties about your unemployment can you turn into prayers today?

Action Step

Create an "Anxiety to Prayer" jar. Write down your anxieties on small slips of paper, pray over them, and place them in the jar as a symbol of giving them to God.

Declarations

- I choose to respond to anxiety with prayer and thanksgiving.
- God cares about my concerns and invites me to bring them to Him.
- As I pray, God's peace guards my heart and mind.

Prayer

Loving Father, I come to You with all my anxieties about unemployment. The uncertainty of my situation often overwhelms me, but I thank You that I can bring all my concerns to You. Help me to resist the urge to worry and instead turn to You in prayer.

When anxious thoughts come, remind me to make my requests known to You. Give me the faith to trust that You hear me and care deeply about my situation. Thank You for Your invitation to cast all my anxieties on You because You care for me.

Lord, I also want to thank You for Your faithfulness, even in this challenging season. Thank You for [name specific blessings]. As I combine my requests with thanksgiving, fill me with Your peace that surpasses all understanding.

In Jesus name I pray, Amen.

Mastering the 24/7 Hustle

"So be careful how you live. Don't live like fools, but like those who are wise. Make the most of every opportunity in these evil days." (Ephesians 5:15-16, NLT)

When you're unemployed, time can feel like both your best friend and your worst enemy. On the one hand, you have more of it. On the other hand, the pressure to "make the most of it" can be overwhelming. It's tempting to fall into one of two extremes: frantically filling every moment with job-search activities or letting time slip away aimlessly.

This scripture calls us to a balanced approach; to walk wisely and make the best use of our time. But what does that look like in the context of unemployment? It means being intentional about how you spend your days. It's about creating a rhythm that includes job searching, skill development, rest, and spiritual growth.

Living wisely in this season means recognizing that "making the most of every opportunity" isn't only about productivity. You are doing more than looking for a job. Maximizing opportunities means aligning your days with God's purposes and using this time to grow in character, deepen your faith, and prepare for the future God has for you.

The phrase "in these evil days" reminds us that we live in a challenging world. Unemployment can feel like a particularly dark season. But it's in these very days that we have the opportunity to shine brightly, using our time in ways that glorify God and bless others.

Challenge yourself to view time as a gift from God, to be stewarded wisely. Create a structure that honors God and serves your long-term growth, not just your immediate employment needs.

Reflection

How can you structure your days to reflect a wise use of time that honors God?

Action Step

Create a weekly schedule that balances job search activities with other essential areas of your life, including spiritual growth, relationships, and self-care.

Declarations

- I choose to use my time wisely in ways that honor God and serve His purposes.
- My days are opportunities for growth, not just in my career but in all areas of life.
- God is guiding me to make the most of this season according to His will.

Prayer

Heavenly Father, thank You for the gift of time. In this season of unemployment, help me to use it wisely and intentionally. Guide me in creating a healthy rhythm for my days. Show me how to balance my job search with other essential aspects of life.

Give me discernment to know when to work hard and when to rest, when to persist, and when to pause. Help me see the opportunities for growth and service that You're placing before me. May my use of time reflect Your wisdom and bring glory to Your name.

Lord, I want to make the best use of this time according to Your purposes. Help me see beyond finding a job to becoming who You're calling me to be. May each day be an opportunity to grow closer to You and to prepare for the future You have planned.

In Jesus name I pray, Amen.

Building Your Bounce-Back Muscles

"And not only that, but we also glory in tribulations, knowing that tribulation produces perseverance; and perseverance, character; and character, hope." (Romans 5:3-4, NKJV)

The journey of unemployment lands punches like a heavyweight boxing match. Rejected applications, unanswered emails, and dwindling savings can feel like a blow to your confidence and hope. But what if these challenges are actually your training ground for resilience?

This scripture presents a powerful progression: tribulation leads to perseverance, which builds character, which ultimately produces hope. It's like a spiritual workout routine for your soul. Each challenge you face is an opportunity to develop your bounce-back muscles.

Your response to these difficulties is critical to your results. Instead of being crushed by challenges, view them as resistance training for your faith and character. Each setback is a chance to practice perseverance. Each disappointment is an opportunity to deepen your trust in God.

Embracing adversity doesn't mean you have to enjoy the hardships. The apostle Paul talks about "glorying" in tribulations not because they feel good but because of what they produce in us. It's about recognizing the value in the struggle, knowing it's shaping you into a stronger, more resilient person.

When you face a challenge in your job search or financial situation, pause and ask yourself: "How can this build my resilience? What can I learn from this?" By reframing difficulties as growth opportunities, you're not just enduring unemployment; you're using it as a launchpad for personal and spiritual development.

Reflection

How have past challenges in your life built resilience that's helping you now?

Action Step

Start a "Resilience Journal." For each setback you face, write down what you learned and how it's making you stronger.

Declarations

- Every challenge I face is building my spiritual and emotional strength.
- I choose to view setbacks as opportunities for growth and character development.
- God is using this season to cultivate endurance, character, and hope in me.

Prayer

Heavenly Father, I confess that the challenges of unemployment often feel overwhelming. Thank You for Your promise that these difficulties can produce endurance, character, and hope in my life. Give me the strength to persevere through each setback.

Help me see the growth opportunities in every challenge I face. Build my resilience muscles, Lord, so I can bounce back stronger from every disappointment. Use this season to shape my character and deepen my faith.

Father, let hope rise within me as I see Your faithfulness in my struggles. May my response to these challenges bring glory to Your name. Help me encourage others with the strength and hope You're cultivating in me through this journey.

In Jesus name I pray, Amen.

Your Spiritual Dream Team

"And let us consider how to inspire each other to greater love and to righteous deeds, not forgetting to gather as a community, as some have forgotten, but encouraging each other, especially as the day of his return approaches." (Hebrews 10:24-25, TPT)

When unemployed, it's easy to feel like you're facing the world alone. The temptation to isolate can be intense, especially if you feel embarrassed about your situation. But now, more than ever, you need your spiritual dream team around you.

This scripture reminds us of the power of community. God calls us to gather together, actively encourage, and spur one another toward love and good deeds. Your community, whether it's your church, a small group, or a few close Christian friends, can be a source of strength, wisdom, and practical support during this challenging time.

Your spiritual dream team isn't just there to make you feel better (although that's important too). Your team helps you grow, challenges you when needed, prays with and for you, and reminds you of God's faithfulness when you're struggling to see it.

The phrase "as the day of his return approaches" adds urgency to this call for community. It reminds us that our time here is limited, and we need each other to stay focused on what truly matters. In the context of unemployment, your spiritual community can help you keep your eyes on eternal values even as you navigate temporal challenges.

Resist the urge to go it alone. Reach out to your spiritual community. Be honest about your struggles and be open to their support. Remember, you have something to offer, too. Your experience just might be what someone else needs to hear.

Reflection

Who are the key players on your spiritual dream team, and how can you engage with them more intentionally during this season?

Action Step

Schedule a coffee date or virtual meetup with a trusted Christian friend or mentor to share your journey and receive encouragement.

Declarations

- I am not alone in this journey; God has provided me with a spiritual community.
- I choose to be open and vulnerable with my trusted Christian friends.
- As I receive support from others, God is equipping me to encourage someone else.

Prayer

Loving Father, thank You for the gift of the Christian community. In this season of unemployment, help me resist the temptation to isolate. Guide me to the right people who can encourage, pray for, and spur me on toward love and good deeds.

Give me the courage to be honest about my struggles and the humility to receive support from others. Show me how I can encourage others, even amid my own challenges. Use this season to deepen my connections within my spiritual family.

Lord, remind me that I'm not alone on this journey. Help me to be vulnerable with my trusted Christian friends and to lean on the strength of my spiritual dream team. As I receive support, equip me to offer encouragement to someone else who might be struggling.

In Jesus name I pray, Amen.

Leveling Up in Life

"Do not despise these small beginnings, for the Lord rejoices to see the work begin," (Zechariah 4:10a, NLT)

Unemployment plunges you into a space that feels stagnant or backward-moving. But what if this time is actually your opportunity to level up in life? This verse reminds us that God values the small beginnings, the seemingly insignificant steps we take toward growth and progress.

Every new skill you learn, every connection you make, and every moment you spend in prayer or self-reflection are part of your personal growth journey. These experiences might seem unimportant or unrelated to your job search, but they're building blocks for your future.

God rejoices to see the work begin. He's not waiting for you to land the perfect job before He starts celebrating your progress. He's cheering you on with every small step you take. This perspective can transform how you view your daily efforts during unemployment.

Consider each day an opportunity to make progress, no matter how small. Maybe you'll learn a new software skill, reach out to a potential mentor, or spend time in prayer and Bible study. Each action is a step forward, a small beginning that God celebrates.

Embrace the journey of growth, even when the destination isn't clear. Trust that God is using this time to prepare you for future opportunities. Your faithfulness in these small beginnings lays the foundation for bigger things to come.

Reflection

What small steps can you take today to invest in your personal or professional growth?

Action Step

Choose one skill related to your desired career field and spend at least thirty minutes today learning or practicing it.

Declarations

- Every small step I take is moving me forward in God's plan.
- I am constantly growing and improving, even in this season of unemployment.
- God rejoices over my efforts to develop myself, no matter how small they seem.

Prayer

Heavenly Father, thank You for valuing even the smallest beginnings in my life. Help me to see this time of unemployment as an opportunity for growth and development. Give me the wisdom to identify areas where I can improve and the discipline to take consistent steps toward progress.

Lord, open my eyes to the opportunities for learning and growth surrounding me. Help me steward this time well, developing skills and habits that will serve me in the future You have planned. When I feel discouraged by slow progress, remind me that You rejoice to see the work begin.

May I never despise these small beginnings but instead celebrate each step forward. Let my growth in this season be a testament to Your faithfulness and transforming power in my life. Thank You for Your patience with my process and Your joy in my journey.

In Jesus name I pray, Amen.

God's Perfect Timing in an Instant World

"But do not forget this one thing, dear friends: With the Lord a day is like a thousand years, and a thousand years are like a day." (2 Peter 3:8, NIV)

In our fast-paced, instant-gratification world, waiting for a job can feel like an eternity. We want results now: the perfect job offers, financial stability, and a clear career path. But God's timeline often looks different from ours.

This verse reminds us that God's perception of time vastly differs from ours. What seems like an agonizingly long wait to us might be just a moment in God's grand plan. His timing doesn't mean He is slow or indifferent to our needs. Instead, it suggests that He's working on a scale we can't always see or understand.

During this waiting period, God might be aligning your circumstances, preparing people, or working in your own heart. He's not wasting time. He's making every moment count in ways we may not recognize yet.

This perspective can help us approach our job search with patience and trust. Instead of frantically trying to force outcomes, we can rest in knowing God is orchestrating events according to His perfect timing.

Today, instead of focusing on the wait, try to shift your perspective to see this time as purposeful preparation. Trust that God's timing is perfect, even when it doesn't match your preferred schedule. He's never late, and He's never early, either. He's always right on time.

Reflection

How might God be using this waiting period to prepare you for what's ahead?

Action Step

Create a "Waiting Well" journal. Each day, write down one way you're growing or one thing you're learning during this time of waiting.

Declarations

- I trust in God's perfect timing for my life and career.
- This waiting period is not wasted time but purposeful preparation.
- God is working behind the scenes, even when I can't see immediate results.

Prayer

Heavenly Father, in this world of instant gratification, help me to trust in Your perfect timing. When I grow impatient with the job search process, remind me that Your perception of time differs from mine. Give me faith to believe You are working even when I can't see immediate results.

Lord, grant me patience and perseverance. When impatience tempts me to rush ahead or force outcomes, help me wait on Your timing. Show me how to be productive and purposeful in this season of preparation. Help me use this time wisely, growing in character and deepening my relationship with You.

Thank You for Your promise to make all things beautiful in Your time. Help me trust in Your wisdom and Your love for me. May my attitude during this waiting period testify to Your goodness and faithfulness.

In Jesus name I pray, Amen.

Flipping the Script on Negativity

"Summing it all up, friends, I'd say you'll do best by filling your minds and meditating on things true, noble, reputable, authentic, compelling, gracious, the best, not the worst; the beautiful, not the ugly; things to praise, not things to curse." (Philippians 4:8, MSG)

Unemployment can be a breeding ground for negative thoughts. It's easy to get caught in a cycle of self-doubt, worry, and pessimism. But today's verse challenges us to flip the script on negativity and intentionally focus our minds on what is good and true.

This scripture doesn't suggest ignoring the challenges of your situation or pretending everything is perfect. Instead, it's about consciously choosing to dwell on the positive aspects of your life and the truth of God's promises, even in challenging circumstances.

When negative thoughts creep in, use this verse as a filter. Is the thought true? Is it noble? Is it reputable? If not, actively replace it with something that is. Maybe it's a truth from Scripture, a memory of God's past faithfulness, or a current blessing in your life.

This practice of positive focus isn't just feel-good psychology; it's a spiritual discipline that can transform your outlook on and experience of unemployment. By filling your mind with good things, you're creating an environment where faith can flourish and resilience can grow.

Challenge yourself to be intentional about your thought life. Whenever you think negatively about your job situation, pause and redirect your mind to something true, noble, reputable, authentic, compelling, or gracious. It might feel unnatural initially, but with practice, it can transform your outlook.

Reflection

What negative thought patterns about your unemployment do you need to challenge and replace?

Action Step

Create a "Positivity Playlist" of truths, promises, and blessings you can review whenever negative thoughts threaten to overwhelm you.

Declarations

- I choose to focus on what is true, noble, and right, even in challenging circumstances.
- My thoughts shape my reality, so I commit to thinking positively and hopefully.
- God's truth is more powerful than my negative thoughts or circumstances.

Prayer

Heavenly Father, in this season of unemployment where negativity can easily creep in, I ask for Your help guarding my thoughts. Thank You for the guidance in Your Word about what to focus my mind on. When doubts, fears, or negative self-talk threaten to overwhelm me, remind me to filter my thoughts through Your truth.

Lord, renew my mind daily. Help me see the good in this situation, recognize Your blessings, and hold onto hope. When my discouragement tempts me to dwell on my circumstances, redirect my focus to Your unchanging character and promises. Show me how to replace negative thoughts with truths from Your Word.

May my thought life be a testimony to Your transforming power. Let my positive outlook in the face of challenges be a witness of Your goodness and faithfulness to others. Thank You for the power to choose my focus.

In Jesus name I pray, Amen.

Money Matters: Divine Edition

"So above all, constantly seek God's kingdom and his righteousness, then all these less important things will be given to you abundantly." (Matthew 6:33, TPT)

Money worries consume your thoughts during unemployment. Bills pile up, savings dwindle, and the future looks uncertain. This scripture offers a radical shift in perspective: seek first God's kingdom and His righteousness, and everything else will fall into place.

Seeking God's righteousness is not a license to ignore our financial responsibilities or stop looking for work. Rather, we must prioritize our relationship with God and align our lives with His will above all else. When we do this, we gain His perspective on our needs and provisions.

Seeking God's kingdom means pursuing His purposes and values in every area of our lives, including our finances and careers. His righteousness refers to right living according to God's standards. As we focus on these, God promises to provide for our needs.

Shift your focus today from financial concerns to seeking God's kingdom. How can you align your job search, use of time, and monetary decisions with God's purposes? Trust that as you prioritize His kingdom, He will take care of the other areas of your life.

Reflection

How might your approach to unemployment change if you focused primarily on seeking God's kingdom?

Action Step

Identify one way you can actively seek God's kingdom today despite your unemployment situation.

Declarations

- I choose to seek God's kingdom first, trusting Him to provide for my needs.
- My primary focus is aligning my life with God's purposes, not just finding a job.
- As I pursue God's righteousness, He abundantly supplies all I need.

Prayer

Heavenly Father, in this time of financial uncertainty, I thank You for Your promise to provide as I seek Your kingdom first. Help me prioritize Your purposes and values above my own concerns and worries. Show me how to align my job search and financial decisions with Your will.

Lord, when anxiety about money creeps in, remind me to refocus on You and Your righteousness. Give me wisdom to manage the resources You've given me and faith to trust in Your provision. Help me to see opportunities to advance Your kingdom, even in this season of unemployment.

Thank You for Your promise of abundant provision. As I seek You first, open my eyes to see the ways You're already providing for me. May my trust in Your care be a testimony to others of Your faithfulness.

In Jesus name I pray, Amen.

Riding the Waves of Change

"There is a season (a time appointed) for everything and a time for every delight and event or purpose under heaven, "
(Ecclesiastes 3:1, AMP)

Change sweeps through life during unemployment, disrupting the steady rhythm of familiar routines. The steady rhythm of your work life is disrupted, and you find yourself navigating unfamiliar waters. This scripture reminds us that change is not just inevitable; it's part of God's design for our lives.

This scripture tells us that there are seasons to life. Just as nature moves through cycles of growth, harvest, rest, and renewal, so do our lives. Your current season of unemployment is not a mistake or a dead end. It's a transition, a time of change with a purpose.

Perhaps this is a season for rest after years of hard work. Maybe it's a time for reassessment of your career goals. It could be a period of preparation for something new. Whatever it is, God is in control of the seasons of your life.

Recognizing that this is a season can bring comfort. Seasons are temporary; they come and go. This difficult time will not last forever. But seasons are also purposeful. Each one plays a crucial role in the overall cycle of growth and development.

Instead of resisting the changes you're experiencing, embrace them as part of your journey. Ask God to show you the purpose in this season and to help you make the most of it. Remember, no season lasts forever. This too shall pass and make way for a new chapter in your life.

Reflection

What might God be trying to teach you or prepare you for in this season of change?

Action Step

Create a "Seasons of Life" timeline. Mark significant changes in your past and note what you learned or how you grew through each transition.

Declarations

- This season of unemployment is temporary and has a purpose.
- I embrace change as an opportunity for growth and new beginnings.
- God is in control of the seasons of my life, including this one.

Prayer

Heavenly Father, as I navigate the choppy waters of unemployment and change, I thank You for the assurance that there is a time and season for everything under Heaven. Help me trust in Your perfect timing and purposes. When I feel overwhelmed by the changes in my life, remind me that You are constant and unchanging.

Lord, grant me wisdom to discern the purpose of this season. If it's a time for rest, help me truly to rest in You. If it's a time for preparation, show me how to prepare. If it's a time for reassessment, guide my thoughts and plans. Give me the courage to embrace this season rather than resist it.

Thank You that no season lasts forever. Give me hope for the future and patience for the present. May I emerge from this season of change stronger in faith and closer to You. Let my response to this time of transition be a testimony to Your faithfulness.

In Jesus name I pray, Amen.

The Dignity of All Work

"Work willingly at whatever you do, as though you were working for the Lord rather than for people." (Colossians 3:23, NLT)

When you're unemployed, it's easy to fall into the trap of thinking only certain jobs have value or dignity. You might find yourself turning down opportunities because they're not in your field or at your desired level. But today's verse challenges us to see all work through God's eyes.

This scripture doesn't distinguish between types of work. Whether you're a CEO or a street sweeper, a brain surgeon or a barista, the calling is the same: work with all your heart, as if you're working directly for God. This perspective imbues all honest work with dignity and purpose.

During your job search, you might need to take on temporary or part-time work outside your career path. Remember, there's no such thing as "just a job" in God's economy. Every task done with excellence and a heart of service is an act of worship.

This mindset can transform how you approach your job search and any work you do in the meantime. It's not about the prestige of the position or the size of the paycheck. It's about the attitude of your heart and the quality of your effort.

View every task as a chance to glorify God. Whether volunteering, managing household chores, or in a temporary job, tackle it with the commitment you would bring to your ideal career. Your attitude and effort can serve as a strong witness, potentially opening unexpected doors.

Reflection

How might your job search or approach to work change if you viewed all tasks as working directly for God?

Action Step

Choose one task today, whether it's a household chore, a volunteer opportunity, or a job application, and do it with exceptional care and effort, as if you were doing it directly for God.

Declarations

- All honest work has dignity because it's an opportunity to serve God.
- I approach every task, big or small, as working for the Lord.
- My attitude and effort in my work are a testimony to my faith.

Prayer

Heavenly Father, thank You for the reminder that all work can be done for Your glory. Help me see the dignity in every task, recognizing that I'm serving You when I work with excellence. As I search for employment, guide me to opportunities where I can use my gifts and skills.

Lord, when my unmet preferences tempt me to grumble about a job or to give less than my best effort, remind me of Your presence in my work. May my attitude and diligence be a witness to Your transforming power in my life to others. Give me the humility to accept and excel in work that might not seem ideal.

Thank You for the gift of work and the ability to contribute to society. Help me find joy and purpose in whatever tasks come my way, knowing that in serving others, I'm serving You. May my work ethic always bring honor to Your name.

In Jesus name I pray, Amen.

Navigating Family Dynamics

"Make allowance for each other's faults, and forgive anyone who offends you. Remember, the Lord forgave you, so you must forgive others." (Colossians 3:13, NLT)

Unemployment doesn't just affect you; it impacts your entire family. Financial stress, changing routines, and shifting dynamics can strain even the strongest relationships. You might feel guilty for not providing, frustrated by a lack of understanding, or hurt by well-meaning but insensitive comments from family members.

Today's verse reminds us of the importance of patience, understanding, and forgiveness in our relationships, especially during challenging times. "Bearing with one another" means showing patience and tolerance, even when tensions are high. Forgiveness becomes crucial when misunderstandings or harsh words threaten to create rifts.

Remember, your family is likely struggling to adjust to this new reality, too. They may not always know how to support you or express their concerns. The call to forgive "as Christ forgave you" sets a high standard, one of unconditional love and grace.

Forgiveness doesn't mean ignoring real issues or allowing harmful behavior. It's about approaching family interactions with an extra measure of grace and understanding. Look for ways to communicate openly, listen empathetically, and forgive quickly.

Embrace the role of grace initiator in your family. This challenging period can strengthen your family bonds if navigated with love and understanding. Allow your unemployment to become a catalyst for your family to grow closer, support one another, and demonstrate Christlike love in practical ways.

Reflection

How can you show more understanding and forgiveness to your family members during this challenging time?

Action Step

Have an open, honest conversation with a family member about how unemployment is affecting you and listen to their perspective as well.

Declarations

- I choose to extend grace and forgiveness to my family, even when it's difficult.
- This challenging season is an opportunity for our family to grow stronger together.
- I will communicate openly and listen empathetically to my family members.

Prayer

Heavenly Father, thank You for the gift of family. During this challenging time of unemployment, help me navigate family dynamics with grace, patience, and love. Give me the strength to bear with my family members, even when tensions are high.

Lord, when misunderstandings occur, or harsh words are spoken, grant me the courage to forgive quickly, just as You have forgiven me. Help me communicate openly and honestly with my family about my struggles and needs. Give me ears to truly listen to their concerns as well.

Use this season to draw our family closer together and closer to You. When I'm tempted to withdraw or lash out in frustration, remind me of Your love and patience toward me. May our family be a testimony to Your grace and love, even in difficult times.

In Jesus name I pray, Amen.

The Waiting Game: God's Perspective

"but those who trust in the Lord will renew their strength; they will soar on wings like eagles; they will run and not become weary, they will walk and not faint." (Isaiah 40:31, CSB)

The job search can unfold like a marathon without a visible finish line. The constant cycle of applications, interviews, and rejections can be exhausting. It's easy to grow weary and lose heart. But today's verse offers a powerful promise for those in the waiting game.

This scripture doesn't just tell us to wait; it tells us to trust in the Lord. Unlike passive wishful thinking, waiting is an active, expectant trust in God's character and promises. As we trust Him, He promises to renew our strength.

The imagery is striking, as it includes soaring like eagles, running without weariness, and walking without fainting. This is God's vision for you in the waiting period. Replace frantic activity with the strength and endurance that comes from above.

Waiting with trust means continuing to take action in your job search but doing so from a place of peace and confidence in God's provision. It means persevering in the face of setbacks, knowing that God is working even when you can't see it.

Shift your focus from the weariness of waiting to the promise of renewal. Instead of obsessing over when your wait will end, ask God how He wants to strengthen and prepare you during this time. Let your waiting become a period of spiritual soaring, where you gain new perspectives and draw closer to God.

Reflection

How can you actively place your trust in God rather than in job prospects today?

Action Step

Set aside time for a "spiritual flight", a period of prayer and worship where you focus on God's character and promises, allowing Him to lift your perspective above your current circumstances.

Declarations

- As I trust in the Lord, He is renewing my strength daily.
- This waiting period is an opportunity to soar spiritually and gain new perspectives.
- God's strength sustains me, even when the job search feels exhausting.

Prayer

Heavenly Father, in this time of waiting for employment, I choose to place my trust firmly in You. When I grow weary of the job search process, remind me of Your promise to renew my strength. Help me soar above my circumstances and gain Your perspective on this season of my life.

Lord, lift my eyes from the immediate challenges to see the bigger picture of what You're doing in and through me. Use this waiting period to deepen my faith, refine my character, and prepare me for the plans You have for me. When I'm tempted to run ahead in my own strength, teach me to wait on You and find supernatural endurance.

Thank You for Your promise that as I hope in You, I will not be disappointed. Give me the courage to keep moving forward, trusting that You are working even when I can't see it. May my patient endurance in this season be a testimony to Your faithfulness.

In Jesus name I pray, Amen.

Redefining Your Win

"I don't think the way you think. The way you work isn't the way I work.' God's Decree. 'For as the sky soars high above earth, so the way I work surpasses the way you work, and the way I think is beyond the way you think." (Isaiah 55:8-9, MSG)

In the world of job hunting, it's easy to define "winning" in precise terms, such as landing the perfect job, achieving a specific salary, or climbing the career ladder. But what if God's definition of success looks different from ours?

Today's scripture reminds us that God's thoughts and ways are far above ours. His plan for your life might not align with societal expectations or even your own career goals. What looks like a setback to you might be a setup for something more significant in God's eyes.

This doesn't mean you should abandon your job search or stop setting goals. Instead, it's an invitation to hold those goals loosely and remain open to God's direction. Success in God's economy might look like personal growth, stronger faith, or opportunities to serve others, even if your employment status hasn't changed yet.

Redefining success according to God's standards can bring freedom and peace. It takes the pressure off you to orchestrate the perfect career move and allows you to trust in God's higher plan. It opens your eyes to see victories you might otherwise miss, like growth in patience, deepening your prayer life, or opportunities to encourage others in their struggles.

Redefine what "winning" looks like in this season. Instead of focusing solely on job outcomes, consider how you're growing in character, deepening your relationship with God, or positively impacting others. These are wins that have eternal value, regardless of your employment status.

Reflection

How might God be defining success for you differently than you've been defining it for yourself?

Action Step

Make a list of "wins" you've experienced during unemployment that aren't related to getting a job, personal growth, stronger relationships, new skills, etc.

Declarations

- I trust that God's plan for my life is higher and better than my own plans.
- I define success by my growth in faith and character, not just by my job status.
- I'm becoming more aligned with God's purposes every day, even if I can't see it yet.

Prayer

Heavenly Father, thank You for the reminder that Your thoughts and ways are higher than mine. Help me trust in Your plan, even when it doesn't align with my expectations or the world's definition of success. Give me the wisdom to see beyond my immediate circumstances and recognize the ways You're working in my life.

Lord, show me how to redefine winning according to Your standards. Help me celebrate growth in character, deepening faith, and opportunities to serve others. Give me eyes to see the victories You're orchestrating, even in this challenging season. When I'm tempted to measure my worth by my job status or income, redirect my focus to the eternal values You prioritize.

Thank You for Your perfect plan for my life. Help me hold my own plans loosely and remain open to Your direction. May my definition of success align more and more with Your perspective.

In Jesus name I pray, Amen.

Bouncing Back from the "No"

"We are troubled on every side, yet not distressed; we are perplexed, but not in despair; Persecuted, but not forsaken; cast down, but not destroyed." (2 Corinthians 4:8-9, TPT)

In the job search process, hearing "no" is often part of the journey. Whether it's a rejected application, a failed interview, or a rescinded offer, each "no" can feel like a blow to your confidence and hope. But today's verse reminds us that, as believers, we have an incredible capacity for resilience.

Paul's words paint a picture of someone facing immense challenges yet remaining undefeated. This resilience doesn't come from our own strength but from the power of Christ within us. Each "no" might trouble or perplex us, but it doesn't have to crush our spirits or destroy our hope.

Bouncing back from rejection is a skill, and like any skill, it improves with practice. Each "no" is an opportunity to exercise your faith, reaffirm your identity in Christ, and lean into God's strength. It's a chance to demonstrate that a job offer doesn't determine your worth. Your status as a child of God makes you worthy.

If you're facing a "no" or the memory of past rejections, remind yourself of who you are in Christ. You are not distressed, not in despair, not forsaken, and certainly not destroyed. Let each setback become a setup for a stronger comeback.

Reflection

How can you reframe your most recent job search "no" as an opportunity for growth or redirection?

Action Step

Write a "Resilience Resume" by listing the setbacks you've overcome in the past and the strengths you've developed through those experiences.

Declarations

- I am resilient because Christ's power works within me.
- Each "no" in my job search is redirecting me to God's better "yes."
- I choose to bounce back stronger after every setback.

Prayer

Heavenly Father, thank You for the resilience You provide in the face of rejection and disappointment. When I feel pressed on every side by job search challenges, remind me that in You, I cannot be crushed. Give me the strength to bounce back from every "no" I encounter.

Help me see rejections not as final verdicts on my worth but as redirections toward Your perfect plan. When perplexed by unanswered applications or failed interviews, guard me from falling into despair. Renew my hope and confidence after each setback.

Lord, use every "no" to refine my character, strengthen my faith, and align me more closely with Your will. Thank You that in You, I am never abandoned or destroyed, no matter how many rejections I face. May my resilience in the face of job search challenges testify to Your sustaining power.

In Jesus name I pray, Amen.

Finding Joy in the Journey

"Consider it nothing but joy, my brothers and sisters, whenever you fall into various trials. Be assured that the testing of your faith [through experience] produces endurance [leading to spiritual maturity, and inner peace]." (James 1:2-3, AMP)

Unemployment drains the vibrancy from daily life, leaving behind a colorless routine. Financial worries, repeated rejections, and uncertainty about the future can drain the happiness out of life. This scripture challenges us to do something that seems counterintuitive: to find joy in our trials.

Finding joy doesn't mean we have to be happy about being unemployed. Rather, it's about recognizing the value and purpose of our struggles. James tells us that these trials test our faith and that test produces endurance, a quality that will serve us well beyond our current circumstances.

Joy, in this context, isn't a fleeting emotion based on our situation. It's a deep-seated attitude from understanding God's work in our lives. It's the ability to see beyond our immediate struggles to the character and faith being forged through them.

The amplified version adds that this endurance leads to spiritual maturity and inner peace. These are priceless qualities that can't be gained through easy times alone. Your current trial is not just a hurdle to overcome but a tool God is using to shape you.

Find moments of joy in your journey. Maybe it's gratitude for unexpected free time, appreciation for supportive friends and family, or excitement about a new skill you're developing. Let joy be your act of faith, declaring that you trust God's work in your life, even in this challenging season.

Reflection

What unexpected blessings or growth opportunities can you identify in your unemployment journey?

Action Step

Start a "Joy Journal." Each day, write down at least one thing that brought you joy or a lesson you're grateful to be learning through this experience.

Declarations

- I choose joy, knowing God is using this trial to strengthen my faith.
- My circumstances don't dictate my joy; my joy comes from the Lord.
- This journey is producing endurance in me, preparing me for future blessings.

Prayer

Loving Father, I confess that finding joy in this season of unemployment is challenging. Thank You for Your Word, which reminds me to consider my trials as opportunities for growth and joy. Help me see beyond my immediate circumstances to the work You're doing in my life.

Lord, produce in me the endurance that comes from tested faith. Give me the strength to choose joy even on difficult days. Help me find delight in Your presence and peace in Your promises. When I'm tempted to focus on the negatives, open my eyes to the blessings and growth opportunities hidden in this journey.

Thank You for walking with me through this valley. May the joy I cultivate in this challenging time be a powerful testimony of Your goodness and faithfulness to others. Use this journey to prepare me for Your plans for my future.

In Jesus name I pray, Amen.

Networking with Purpose

"Two people are better off than one, for they can help each other succeed. If one person falls, the other can reach out and help. But someone who falls alone is in real trouble."
(Ecclesiastes 4:9-10, NLT)

In today's job market, we often hear, "It's not what you know but who you know." Networking has become a crucial part of job searching, but for many, it can feel uncomfortable or self-serving. Today's scripture, however, gives us a different perspective on the power of connections.

This passage emphasizes the value of partnership and mutual support. In God's economy, networking isn't about using people for personal gain; it's about building genuine relationships where we can support and uplift one another. It's about creating a community where, when one falls (perhaps through job loss), others are there to help them up.

The beauty of this approach is that it's not just about what others can do for you but also how you can contribute to others' success. Even in your unemployment, you have valuable experiences, insights, and abilities that can help someone else.

As you network during your job search, shift your mindset from "What can this person do for me?" to "How can we support each other?" Look for opportunities to add value to others, even as you seek help for yourself. This approach aligns with God's principles and often leads to more meaningful and fruitful connections.

Network with purpose today. Reach out to someone not just for a job lead but to genuinely connect, encourage, or offer support. Remember, the relationships you build now may be the ones that help you up when you fall or allow you to lift someone else in the future.

Reflection

How can you approach networking in a way that focuses on mutual support rather than personal gain?

Action Step

Reach out to three people in your network today. Instead of asking for job leads, ask how you can support or encourage them in their current endeavors.

Declarations

- I build relationships with genuine care and a desire for mutual support.
- God is connecting me with the right people at the right time.
- I add value to others' lives, even as I seek support in my own journey.

Prayer

Heavenly Father, thank You for the gift of community and the power of supportive relationships. As I network during my job search, help me to do so with purpose and genuine care for others. Guide me to the right connections and give me wisdom in building meaningful relationships.

Lord, show me how I can add value to others' lives, even in my own time of need. When my needs tempt me to focus solely on my own goals, remind me of the importance of lifting others up. Give me the courage to be vulnerable and the strength to support others in their struggles.

Thank You for the people You've placed in my life. Help me to be a good steward of these relationships, using them not just for my benefit but for the good of others and the advancement of Your kingdom. May my networking efforts reflect Your love and bring glory to Your name.

In Jesus name I pray, Amen.

Overcoming Self-Doubt

"For God has not given us a spirit of fear, but of power and of love and of a sound mind." (2 Timothy 1:7, NKJV)

Unemployment can be a breeding ground for self-doubt. As rejections pile up or the job search drags on, you might find yourself questioning your skills, your worth, or your future. Thoughts like "Maybe I'm not good enough" or "What if I never find a job?" can become unwelcome companions.

But today's verse reminds us that these doubts and fears don't come from God. Instead, He's given us a spirit of power, love, and a sound mind (or self-discipline). In Christ, you have the power to overcome self-doubt, the love to affirm your worth in God's eyes, and the mental clarity to approach your situation with wisdom and confidence.

The power God gives us is not just for big, dramatic moments. It's an everyday power that enables us to face challenges, including job searches, with courage and resilience. His love reminds us that our worth is not tied to our employment status but to our identity as His beloved children.

A "sound mind" or self-discipline helps us to think clearly and make wise decisions, even when emotions run high. It allows us to separate truth from lies, to focus on facts rather than fears, and to take purposeful action instead of being paralyzed by doubt.

Confront your self-doubt with God's truth today. When negative thoughts arise, counter them with scripture and affirmations of who you are in Christ. Remember, God has given you a spirit of power, love, and a sound mind, use these gifts to combat self-doubt and move forward confidently.

Reflection

What specific self-doubts have you been struggling with, and how can you counter them with God's truth?

Action Step

Create a "Truth vs. Lies" chart. On one side, write down your self-doubts. On the other, write corresponding truths from Scripture that counter these doubts.

Declarations

- I have the power to overcome self-doubt through Christ, who strengthens me.
- God's love for me is not based on my employment status but on His unchanging character.
- I approach my job search with a sound mind, confident in God's guidance.

Prayer

Heavenly Father, thank You for not giving me a spirit of fear but power, love, and a sound mind. When self-doubt creeps in during this season of unemployment, help me to remember who I am in You. Fill me with Your power to overcome negative thoughts and insecurities.

Lord, remind me of Your unconditional love that affirms my worth beyond any job title or salary. Grant me a sound mind to approach my job search with wisdom and confidence. When I'm tempted to question my skills or value, bring Your truth to the forefront of my mind.

Help me see myself as You see me: capable, worthy, and full of potential. Give me the courage to step out in faith, trusting in the gifts and abilities You've given me. May my confidence in You shine through in every application and interview.

In Jesus name I pray, Amen.

The Importance of Self-Care

"Come to me, all you who are weary and burdened, and I will give you rest. Take my yoke upon you and learn from me, for I am gentle and humble in heart, and you will find rest for your souls."
(Matthew 11:28-29, NIV)

The stress of unemployment can take a toll on your physical, emotional, and spiritual well-being. It's easy to fall into the trap of constant job searching, neglecting your own needs in the process. But today's scripture reminds us of the importance of rest and self-care, especially during challenging times.

Jesus invites those who are weary and burdened to come to Him for rest. He isn't just talking about physical rest but a profound, soul-level renewal that comes from connecting with God. Self-care isn't selfish; it's crucial to maintaining your strength and perspective during your job search.

Taking care of yourself involves more than just sleep or relaxation. It includes nurturing your relationship with God, maintaining physical health, cultivating supportive relationships, and engaging in activities that refresh your spirit. When you prioritize self-care, you're better equipped to handle the challenges of unemployment and to recognize opportunities when they arise.

Jesus also invites us to take His yoke and learn from Him. His invitation suggests that proper rest comes not from inactivity but from aligning ourselves with Christ's gentle and humble way. It's about finding the right balance between effort and rest, guided by His wisdom and character.

Give yourself permission to rest and recharge. Accept Jesus's invitation to come to Him and find rest for your soul. Remember, taking care of yourself is an essential part of your job search strategy. It's an investment in your ability to persist and succeed in the long run.

Reflection

What areas of self-care have you been neglecting, and how can you prioritize them?

Action Step

Create a weekly self-care plan that includes spiritual, physical, emotional, and social activities to help you stay balanced and refreshed.

Declarations

- I prioritize self-care as an essential part of my job search strategy.
- In Jesus, I find true rest and renewal for my soul.
- Taking care of myself enables me to approach my job search with energy and clarity.

Prayer

Loving Father, thank You for Your invitation to come to You for rest. In the midst of the stress and uncertainty of unemployment, help me to prioritize self-care and find renewal in Your presence. Guide me in creating healthy habits that nurture my body, mind, and spirit.

Lord, when I overwork or neglect my own needs, remind me of the importance of balance and rest. Show me how to take Your yoke upon me and learn from Your gentle and humble heart. Refresh my soul with Your love and peace.

Help me to engage in activities that bring joy and restoration. Give me wisdom to know when to push forward in my job search and when to step back and recharge. Thank You for caring about every aspect of my well-being. May my commitment to self-care enable me to serve others from a place of strength and wholeness.

In Jesus name I pray, Amen.

Serving Others While Unemployed

"Be generous with the different things God gave you, passing them around so all get in on it." (1 Peter 4:10, MSG)

When you're focused on finding a job, it's easy to become absorbed in your own needs and challenges. But today's verse reminds us that we all have gifts to share, regardless of our employment status. Serving others isn't just for those who have it all together. It's a calling for every believer in every season of life.

Unemployment, while challenging, can provide unique opportunities to serve. You might have more flexible time to volunteer, or your job search skills could help someone else update their résumé. Your experience of unemployment itself might enable you to empathize with and encourage others in similar situations.

The Message's translation emphasizes "passing around" our gifts so everyone benefits. This practice creates a beautiful picture of a community where everyone contributes what they can and meets everyone's needs. Your current situation doesn't disqualify you from this exchange. It might actually give you a unique perspective to offer.

Serving isn't just about what you do for others; it also has profound benefits for you. It can help shift your focus from your own problems, provide a sense of purpose, and even open up unexpected networking opportunities. Most importantly, it allows you to be a faithful steward of God's grace, even in this challenging season.

Look for ways to use your gifts to serve others. It might be through formal volunteering, helping a neighbor, or encouraging a fellow job seeker. Remember, your ability to serve isn't defined by your job title but by your identity in Christ.

Reflection

What unique gifts or experiences do you have that could be used to serve others during this time of unemployment?

Action Step

Find one way to serve someone else today, whether through a small act of kindness or by volunteering your skills to help another person or organization.

Declarations

- I am equipped to serve others, regardless of my employment status.
- Serving others brings purpose and perspective to my own journey.
- I am a faithful steward of God's grace, even in this season of unemployment.

Prayer

Loving Father, thank You for the gifts and abilities You've given me. Help me see opportunities to use these gifts to serve others, even in this season of unemployment. Open my eyes to the needs around me and show me how I can make a difference.

Lord, when I'm tempted to focus solely on my own situation, remind me of the joy and purpose found in serving others. Use my experiences, both the challenges and the blessings, to encourage and support those around me. Help me to be a faithful steward of Your grace, sharing Your love through my actions and words.

Thank You for the opportunity to serve, even when I feel I have little to offer. May my willingness to give of myself be a testimony to Your generous love. Use my service to not only bless others but also to shape me more into the image of Christ.

In Jesus name I pray, Amen.

Staying Motivated in the Job Search

"And don't allow yourselves to be weary or disheartened in planting good seeds, for the season of reaping the wonderful harvest you've planted is coming!" (Galatians 6:9, TPT)

The job search stretches before you like an endless road, testing your endurance with each step forward. Sending out applications, following up on leads, and facing rejections can be exhausting. This scripture offers encouragement to persist, reminding us that our efforts will bear fruit if we don't give up.

In the context of your job search, "planting good seeds" involves more than just applying for jobs. It includes maintaining a positive attitude, developing your skills, networking with integrity, and trusting in God's timing. These actions are like planted seeds. They may not show immediate results, but they are growing beneath the surface.

The promise of reaping a "wonderful harvest" reminds us that our efforts are not in vain. Your ideal job opportunity may not have opened up yet, or you may still be developing the skills or character needed for your next role. Trust that God is working behind the scenes, orchestrating circumstances for your good.

This verse also acknowledges the reality of weariness and discouragement. These feelings are normal, but we're encouraged not to allow them to dominate us. Instead, we're called to persevere with hope and expectation.

Choose to renew your motivation today. Approach your job search activities with fresh energy and hope. Remember, every application, every networking conversation, and every skill you develop brings you one step closer to your harvest.

Reflection

What aspects of your job search feel most draining, and how can you approach them with renewed motivation?

Action Step

Set small, achievable daily goals for your job search to help maintain momentum and celebrate progress.

Declarations

- I choose to persist in my job search, knowing that my efforts will bear fruit.
- God is working behind the scenes, preparing me for the right opportunity.
- I approach each day of my job search with renewed energy and hope.

Prayer

Heavenly Father, when I grow weary in my job search, remind me of Your promise that I will reap a harvest if I do not give up. Renew my motivation and help me persist in doing good. Give me the strength to continue sending out applications, networking, and developing my skills, even when I don't see immediate results.

Lord, when discouragement tries to set in, fill me with fresh hope and energy. Show me how to break down my job search into manageable tasks so I can celebrate small victories along the way. Help me trust in Your perfect timing, believing You are working all things together for my good.

Thank You for Your faithfulness in every season. Help me see this time not just as a wait for employment but as a period of growth and preparation for the harvest You have planned. May my persistent faith be a testimony to Your sustaining power.

In Jesus name I pray, Amen.

Balancing Persistence and Flexibility

"Therefore see that you walk carefully [living life with honor, purpose, and courage; shunning those who tolerate and enable evil], not as the unwise, but as wise [sensible, intelligent, discerning people], making the very most of your time [on earth, recognizing and taking advantage of each opportunity and using it with wisdom and diligence], because the days are [filled with] evil."
(Ephesians 5:15-16, AMP)

In the job search, there's a delicate balance between the persistent pursuit of your goals and remaining flexible to new opportunities. It's easy to become so focused on a specific job or career path that you miss other doors God might be opening. Today's scripture encourages us to live wisely, making the most of every opportunity.

Being persistent means not giving up on your job search, continuously improving your skills, and following up on leads. Flexibility allows you to recognize and seize unexpected opportunities. When you are open to roles or industries you hadn't considered or been willing to take, you may discover a stepping-stone job that could lead to something greater.

The *Amplified Bible* emphasizes living with honor, purpose, and courage. This command reminds us that how we conduct our job search is just as important as the outcome. Maintaining integrity, staying true to your values, and having the courage to step out of your comfort zone are possible when God leads.

Living wisely in your job search involves discernment, knowing when to push forward and when to pivot. It requires staying attuned to God's guidance and being willing to adjust your plans if He's leading you in a new direction.

Be diligent with your efforts, but remain open to unexpected possibilities. Ask God for wisdom to recognize the opportunities He places in your path, even if they don't look exactly like what you had envisioned.

Reflection

Are there any opportunities you might be overlooking because they don't fit your original job search plan?

Action Step

Explore a job opportunity or skill development path outside your usual focus but aligns with your broader skills and interests.

Declarations

- I balance persistence in my goals with flexibility to God's leading.
- I am open to recognizing and seizing unexpected opportunities.
- God's wisdom guides me in making the most of every opportunity.

Prayer

Heavenly Father, thank You for Your guidance in my job search. Grant me the wisdom to live carefully, balancing persistence with flexibility as I seek employment. Help me be diligent in pursuing my goals but also open to new directions You might be leading me.

Lord, give me discernment to recognize the opportunities You're placing in my path, even if they look different from what I expected. When I'm tempted to become rigid in my plans, remind me to seek Your will above my own. Help me make the most of every opportunity, trusting that You can use any experience to prepare me for Your purposes.

Thank You for Your promise of wisdom when I ask for it. May my choices in this job-search journey reflect Your guidance and bring glory to Your name. Help me to step out in faith when You open new doors, knowing that Your plans for me are good.

In Jesus name I pray, Amen.

Breaking Free from the Comparison Trap

"Pay careful attention to your own work, for then you will get the satisfaction of a job well done, and you won't need to compare yourself to anyone else. For we are each responsible for our own conduct." (Galatians 6:4-5, NLT)

In the age of social media, it's easier than ever to fall into the comparison trap. When you're unemployed, seeing updates about others' job successes or career advancements can be particularly challenging. You might find yourself questioning your worth or progress. But today's scripture offers a healthier perspective on self-evaluation.

This passage encourages us to focus on our own actions and progress rather than measuring ourselves against others. Your job-search journey is unique and shaped by your specific skills, circumstances, and God's individual plan for your life. Comparing your chapter one to someone else's chapter twenty isn't fair or helpful.

The satisfaction of a "job well done" comes from knowing you've given your best effort, regardless of the outcome. This concept applies not just to paid work but to how you conduct your job search, develop your skills, and maintain your integrity during unemployment.

Being "responsible for our own conduct" reminds us that we have control over our actions and attitudes, even when we can't control our circumstances. Instead of envying others' successes, we can channel that energy into improving ourselves and doing our best with what we have.

Break free from the comparison trap. Instead of looking at others' successes with envy, use them as inspiration. Focus on your own growth, the lessons you're learning, and the unique ways God is shaping you through this experience.

Reflection

How has comparison affected your job-search journey, and what steps can you take to focus more on your own progress?

Action Step

Create a "Personal Growth Journal" where you regularly note your progress, lessons learned, and small victories in your job search.

Declarations

- I focus on my own growth and progress, not comparing myself to others.
- My worth is not determined by my job status or how I measure up to others.
- I celebrate my own journey, trusting in God's unique plan for my life.

Prayer

Heavenly Father, in a world that constantly invites comparison, help me focus on the unique path You've set before me. When I'm tempted to measure my worth against others' successes, remind me of Your individual love and plan for my life.

Give me the wisdom to evaluate my actions and progress without the distorting lens of comparison. Help me celebrate the growth I'm experiencing and the lessons I'm learning in this season of unemployment. When I see others succeeding, guard my heart against envy and help me to rejoice with them genuinely.

Thank You for the unique ways You're shaping me through this experience. Help me to trust in Your timing and Your plan, knowing that my journey is exactly where it needs to be. May my confidence in Your guidance be a testimony to others.

In Jesus name I pray, Amen.

Prayer

Thank you, Lord, that faith is my response to occasion; help me to ... ... when I respond.

Prepped and Ready for What's Next

> "For I know the plans that I have for you,' declares the Lord, 'plans for welfare and not for calamity to give you a future and a hope."
> (Jeremiah 29:11, NASB)

As your period of unemployment continues, it can be tempting to focus solely on the present challenges. But today's verse reminds us that God has plans for our future, plans filled with hope and welfare. This doesn't necessarily mean material wealth but rather a future where we thrive according to God's purposes.

Believing in God's good plans for your future can transform how you approach your present. Instead of just waiting for a job, you can actively prepare for the opportunities God has in store. Start by developing new skills, deepening your spiritual life, or building relationships that could lead to future opportunities.

The word "welfare" in this verse suggests that God's plans are for your overall well-being, not just your career but your whole life. He sees the bigger picture and is working to align all aspects of your life with His purposes.

Preparing for new opportunities isn't about anxiously trying to control your future. It's about faithfully stewarding your time and talents, trusting that God will open the right doors at the right time. It's about cultivating a spirit of expectancy, knowing God is working behind the scenes.

Take one step toward preparing for your future. Learn a new skill, reach out to a potential mentor, or simply spend time in prayer, asking God to reveal the next step in His plan for you.

Reflection

What skills or qualities might you need to develop to be ready for the future God has planned for you?

Action Step

Create a "Future Preparation Plan" outlining skills you want to develop, relationships you want to build, and spiritual goals you want to achieve during this season.

Declarations

- God has good plans for my future, filled with hope and purpose.
- I actively prepare for new opportunities, trusting in God's timing.
- Each day brings me closer to the future God has prepared for me.

Prayer

Heavenly Father, thank You for Your promise of a hope-filled future. In this season of unemployment, help me focus less on my present circumstances and more on preparing for the opportunities You have planned for me.

Guide me in using this time wisely. Show me the skills I should develop, the relationships I should nurture, and the spiritual growth I need to pursue. Give me a spirit of expectancy, trusting You are working behind the scenes.

Lord, when doubts creep in about my future, remind me of Your faithfulness and Your good plans for me. Help me see this waiting period as a preparation time for the great things You have in store. Grant me wisdom to recognize the doors You're opening and the courage to walk through them.

In Jesus name I pray, Amen.

Gratitude: Your Secret Weapon

"give thanks in all circumstances; for this is God's will for you in Christ Jesus." (1 Thessalonians 5:18, NIV)

Gratitude seems impossible amid the stark realities of unemployment. Financial stress, rejection, and uncertainty about the future can overshadow any sense of thankfulness. This scripture challenges us to give thanks in all circumstances, not for all circumstances, but in them.

Practicing gratitude during challenging times isn't about denying the reality of your situation. It's about choosing to focus on the blessings that exist alongside the difficulties. It's recognizing God's presence and provision even in the valley.

Gratitude has the power to shift our perspective. It can lift our eyes from our immediate problems to see the bigger picture of God's faithfulness. It can also have practical benefits, such as reducing stress, improving mood, and even making us more attractive to potential employers.

"This is God's will for you" suggests that gratitude is more than a nice idea. Gratitude is a crucial part of our spiritual walk. Being grateful is a discipline that aligns our hearts with God's heart, helping us to trust Him more fully.

Cultivate an attitude of gratitude and actively look for things to be thankful for, no matter how small. It could be the support of a friend, a new skill you've learned, or simply the gift of another day. Let your thanksgiving serve as an act of faith, declaring your trust in God's goodness even when circumstances are challenging.

Reflection

What are three things you can be genuinely thankful for in your current situation?

Action Step

Start a daily gratitude journal. Each day, write down at least three things you're thankful for, no matter how small they might seem.

Declarations

- I choose to give thanks in all circumstances, trusting in God's goodness.
- Gratitude shifts my focus from my problems to God's faithfulness.
- Even in unemployment, I can find reasons to be thankful every day.

Prayer

Heavenly Father, I thank You for Your presence with me in this challenging season of unemployment. Help me cultivate a heart of gratitude, even when my circumstances make it difficult. Open my eyes to see the blessings around me that I might be overlooking.

Lord, use this practice of gratitude to transform my perspective. Let my thankful heart be a testimony to Your goodness and faithfulness. Help me to encourage others through my attitude of gratitude, even in the midst of my struggles.

I choose to trust in Your provision and give thanks in all circumstances, knowing that this is Your will for me in Christ Jesus. May my gratitude draw me closer to You and prepare my heart for the blessings yet to come. Thank You for Your unfailing love and care.

In Jesus name I pray, Amen.

Turning the Page: Your Next Chapter Begins

"Forget about what's happened; don't keep going over old history. Be alert, be present. I'm about to do something brand-new. It's bursting out! Don't you see it? There it is! I'm making a road through the desert, rivers in the badlands."
(Isaiah 43:18-19, MSG)

It's time to look forward with hope and anticipation. Whether you've found employment or are still searching. God is calling you to embrace a new chapter. Today's scripture encourages us not to dwell on the past but to be alert to the new thing God is doing.

This doesn't mean forgetting the lessons learned during your unemployment journey. Rather, it's about not letting past disappointments or failures define your future. God is always at work, making ways where there seems to be no way, bringing life to what seemed barren.

The imagery of a road through the desert and rivers in the badlands is powerful. It suggests that God can bring opportunity out of barrenness and hope out of despair. Your period of unemployment, which may have felt like a desert, could be the very place where God is paving a new road for your future.

Embracing a new chapter requires both faith and action. Being open to new possibilities, stepping out of your comfort zone, and trusting God's guidance are examples of faith in action. You may need to redefine success, explore new career paths, or use your experiences to help others. God's new things might not come in the packages we expect, so we must be attentive to His work in our lives.

Allow yourself to dream again. Ask God to refresh your vision for the future. Be open to the "new thing" He is doing, even if it looks different from what you expected. Remember, your story doesn't end with unemployment, it's just one chapter in the greater narrative God is writing with your life.

Reflection

How has your perspective on work and life changed through this unemployment journey, and how can you carry these lessons into your future?

Action Step

Write a letter to your future self, describing the growth you've experienced and the hopes you have for this new chapter.

Declarations

- I am open to the new things God is doing in my life.
- My past does not define my future; God is making a way for me.
- I step into this new chapter with faith, hope, and expectation.

Prayer

Heavenly Father, thank You for bringing me through this season of unemployment. As I stand on the threshold of a new chapter, help me embrace the future with hope and faith. Give me the courage to let go of past disappointments and failures.

Lord, open my eyes to see the new thing You're doing in my life. When I can't see the way forward, remind me that You're making a way in the wilderness and streams in the wasteland. Renew my dreams and vision for the future. Help me to step out in faith, trusting in Your guidance and provision.

Thank You for Your faithfulness throughout this journey. May this new chapter be marked by a deeper trust in You, a greater awareness of Your presence, and a commitment to use my experiences to bless others. Use all I've learned during this time to prepare me for the plans You have for me.

In Jesus name I pray, Amen.

"I know all about the marvelous destiny I have in store for you, a future planned out in detail. My intention is not to harm you but to surround you with peace and prosperity and to give you a beautiful future, glistening with hope. When you call on me and come to me in prayer, I will listen to your every word. If you reach out to me, you will find me when you search for me with all your heart."

Jeremiah 29:11-13 TPT

About The Author

Jennifer Francis knows firsthand that life's path isn't always straight. After twenty years of climbing the corporate ladder at a Fortune 500 company, she suddenly found herself standing at an unexpected crossroads, jobless and unsure of her next step.

But where others might see an ending, Jennifer saw a beginning.

Uncertain about the future yet unwavering in her faith, Jennifer embraced this new chapter of her life with open arms. As she navigated the uncharted waters of unemployment, she discovered a wellspring of strength in her deepening relationship with God. It was in these quiet moments of reflection and prayer that this devotional was born.

Jennifer's unique journey, from Chief of Staff to entrepreneur to author, infuses her writing with a powerful blend of real-world wisdom and spiritual insight. Her words resonate with anyone facing life's pivotal moments, whether it's an unexpected job loss, a daunting career shift, or any season of unanticipated change.

Through these pages, Jennifer shares a message that's both simple and profound: Your pause has a purpose. With warmth, honesty, and a contemporary voice, she reminds us that God remains faithful and in control even in our most uncertain moments.

This devotional isn't just a book - it's Jennifer's testimony to the power of faith in times of transition. It's an invitation to find hope, purpose, and even joy in life's unexpected pauses. Join Jennifer as she shares the lessons learned from her own career shift and the beautiful truths uncovered in her deepened walk with God.

Remember, your story isn't over. It's just taking an inspired intermission.

www.ingramcontent.com/pod-product-compliance
Lightning Source LLC
Chambersburg PA
CBHW060837050426
42453CB00008B/725